Grieg Masterpieces
for Solo Piano
23 Works

Edvard Grieg

DOVER PUBLICATIONS, INC.
Mineola, New York

Bibliographical Note

This Dover edition, first published in 1999, is a new compilation of works originally published separately by C. F. Peters, Leipzig, n.d.

International Standard Book Number: 0-486-40619-9

Manufactured in the United States of America
Dover Publications, Inc., 31 East 2nd Street, Mineola, N.Y. 11501

CONTENTS

Four Norwegian Dances (Op. 35) 1
    I.   Allegro marcato   1
    II. Allegretto tranquillo e grazioso   9
    III. Allegro moderato alla marcia   12
    IV. Allegro molto   15

Valses-Caprices (Op. 37) 24
    I. In C-sharp Minor   24
    II. In E Minor   30

From Holberg's Time (Suite, Op. 40) 34
    I. Praeludium   34
    II. Sarabande   40
    III. Gavotte   42
    IV. Air   44
    V. Rigaudon   48

Peer Gynt (from Suites, Opp. 46, 55) 51
    I. Morning Mood   51
    II. Åse's Death   56
    III. Anitra's Dance   58
    IV. In the Hall of the Mountain King   62
    V. Solvejg's Song   67

Lyric Pieces (from Opp. 43, 54, 65) 70
    Erotik   70
    March of the Trolls   72
    Notturno   78
    Wedding Day at Troldhaugen   82

Moods (from Op. 73) 92
    Scherzo-Impromptu   92
    Night Ride   96

Sonata in E Minor (Op. 7) 102
    I. Allegro moderato   102
    II. Andante molto   108
    III. Alla Menuetto, ma poco più lento   112
    IV. *Finale:* Molto allegro   114

Four Norwegian Dances

Op. 35 (1881)

Transcribed by the composer from his work for piano four hands

I.

II.

Allegretto tranquillo e grazioso. ♩ = 76

III.

Valses-Caprices
Op. 37 (1883)

Transcribed by the composer from his work for piano four hands

I.

II.

From Holberg's Time
Suite, Op. 40 (1884)
I. Praeludium

II. Sarabande

Andante espressivo ♩ = 52

III. Gavotte

MUSETTE

Un poco più mosso

Gavotte da Capo al Fine

IV. Air

V. Rigaudon

TRIO

Rigaudon da capo al fine, ma senza repetizione.

Peer Gynt

Sections I–IV comprise *Peer Gynt Suite No. 1* (Op. 46, 1874–5, revised 1888)
Transcribed by the composer from his orchestral suite based on incidental music to Ibsen's play, Op. 23

I. Morning Mood

II. Åse's Death

Andante doloroso ♩=50

III. Anitra's Dance

*) The trills without concluding notes.

IV. In the Hall of the Mountain King

Alla marcia e molto marcato ♩ = 138

sempre stretto al fine

V. Solvejg's Song

From *Peer Gynt Suite No. 2* (Op. 55, 1874–5, revised 1891–2)

Transcribed by the composer from his orchestral suite based on incidental music to Ibsen's play, Op. 23

Lyric Pieces
Erotik
Op. 43, No. 5 (1886)

March of the Trolls
Op. 54, No. 3 (1891)

Notturno

Op. 54, No. 4 (1891)

Wedding Day at Troldhaugen

Op. 65, No. 6 (1897)

Tempo di Marcia un poco vivace.

Troldhaugen, site of the composer's country villa.

Moods
Scherzo-Impromptu
Op. 73, No. 2 (1903–5)

Night Ride

Op. 73, No. 3 (1903–5)

*) The melody is to be played by the thumb throughout the passage.

Sonata in E Minor
Op. 7

Sonata in E Minor

Op. 7 (1865, revised 1887)

I.

II.

Andante molto.

III.

Alla Menuetto, ma poco più lento.

Finale.
Molto allegro.

IV.